Truths and Consequences

Truths and Consequences

poems

Lisa E Baldwin

N8tive Run Press

Jerome Prairie, Oregon

Copyright @ 2021 by Lisa E Baldwin

All rights reserved. No part of this book may be reproduced in any form or by any electronic or mechanical means or the facilitation thereof, including information storage and retrieval system, without permission in writing from the publisher, except by a reviewer, who may quote brief passages in a review.

First Printing

ISBN 978-0-578-86670-3

Published by N8tive Run Press

N8tive Run Press
 — a subsidiary of N8tive Run Enterprises
5007 Laurel Avenue
Grants Pass, Oregon 97527

n8tiverun.enterprises@gmail.com

Dedication

Most lovingly, I thank my dear husband, Jack,

for his patience and kind support.

And I give thanks and love to my son, Nicholas,

my one and only, my heart.

Contents

Truths and Consequences

Foreword   7

I. Written Dissections
    Biology   13
    Mrs. Ruby on Playground Duty in May   14
    Moon Mission   16
    KBEX 9663—Do You Copy?   18
    Be A Hero   20
    Early Bloomers   21

II. Bearing Witness
    Witness   25
    Carnival   26
    Note to My Rapist   27
    He Lied   28
    Why I Didn't Report   29
    Lost Things   30
    Draft Field Guide American Girls   31

III. Lessons from the World of Men
    A Tale from the Age of Indecency   35
    Back Word Scenes   37
    Name It   38
    Broken up   39
    Valentine to Myself   40
    How to Poison Your Lover   41
    Survivor   42
    Lessons from the World of Men   43
    Fat Broad   44
    Still   45
    Violence Against Her   46
    Waiting for the Light, I see my Ex   48
    Survival: A Field Guide   49

IV. Mother and Son

Thirty Years On	53
February 13, 1990	55
Existential Trinity	56
For My Fatherless Son	57
What a Woman Bears	58
How It Is	59
Falling	60
An Optimistic Mother	61
For Nick, in your new home	62
Freedom	63

V. Commiserate Hearts

Pity the Women	67
Women's Work:	68
The Sacrifice of Hands	69
Forest Crone	70
Women in the Middle Ages	71
Old Testament: Book of Numbers	72
Terms of Endearment	74
When She Ended	75
To My Mother in room R-11…	76
October 4 in Room R-11	77
Pie	79
Gratitude in 2020	80
Convocation: Women Grieve Together	81
Welcome to a New Daughter	82

VI. The Sky is Sometimes Blue

Tempered Steel	85
Post-Meridian: January 17, 2012	86
Sestina: Leaving a Mark	87
One Chance More	89
Logos	90
I Do	91
Map to You	92
Small Promises	93
Sestina: For Tomorrow	94
Parsing Love	96
Ode for my Working Man's Hands	97
Going Nowhere, gladly	98
Sunday	99
Coming Back	100
A Good Day	101

VII. Being

About Being Connected	105
Tap-Girl Saves the World	106
Identity Crisis	107
Not Forgotten	109
Out West	110
Scarred Heart: Reflections ...	111
A Red Tide Blooms	112
city	113
Ode to the Internet	114
Carpe Diem: Friday, November 13	116
211	117
Directions: Where I Live Now	118
Lightfall	120

Acknowledgements   122
Gratitudes   123
About the Poet   124

Foreword

It is an enormous privilege and pleasure to introduce Lisa Baldwin's first collection of poetry, *Truths and Consequences*. As a friend and enthusiastic supporter, I have looked forward to the moment I could hold a volume of her work in my hand. In its originality, searing intelligence, and sublime use of poetic form, Lisa's voice reminds us of poetry's capacity to speak resistance and spark renewal. But most importantly, Lisa is an accomplished wordsmith who celebrates the beauty of language in its highest form.

One score and six is all we have to perpetually rearrange, poetically remix. This line from the poem, "About Being Connected" illustrates, in the most eloquent way, Lisa's talent as a poet. By confessing that her tools are simple, Lisa underscores the consummate skill with which she wields them.

And wield them, she does. I could characterize Lisa using several different descriptors. As her poems proclaim, Lisa is a poet of the land, and specifically, of the land that is southern Oregon. Populated with the names of the mountains, prairies, creeks and rivers that encompass this unique part of Oregon, Lisa's poetry reveals how this particular geography shapes those who shelter within it. From a girlhood in the shadow of Sloan Mountain to the decades spent in daily worship of life unfolding on Jerome Prairie, Lisa chronicles her experiences. She masterfully weaves the dramas of humankind with intimate observations of the wild beings that visit; the insects, birds, flowers, and trees that inhabit her surroundings; and the seasonal changes that are an intrinsic part of her earthly life.

Secondly, but in no way secondary, Lisa is a feminist poet. Lisa's world is made of strong, sassy, sniveling, tap-dancing, high-heel wearing, watchful, weary, worn-out, wonderful women. Her poetry sings with their stories, criticizes their complacency, applauds their cold-eyed clarity, sends us chilling messages from their captivity by the forces designed to keep them in their place; and then sets them free with her words, with her wisdom, and with her belief in herself and in all other women. In her book The Work of a Common Woman (St. Martin's Press, 1978), the poet Judy Grahn once wrote:

> *the common woman is as common as*
>   *the best of bread*
> *and will rise*
> *and will become strong - I swear it to you*
> *I swear it to you on my own head*
> *I swear it to you on my common*
> *woman's*
> *head**

Lisa celebrates the rising of that woman, of everywoman who stumbles through adolescence, loses herself in the trappings of marriage, births a son, buries parents and others, and within all of it, and through all of it, reaches deep to remain loyal to herself. As the voice of that common woman, Lisa becomes an unflinching poet, a poet whose words shatter illusions while speaking truths. Her poems give shelter while the storm rages.

    In the days leading up to January 6th, 2021, I had immersed myself in editing this collection of Lisa's poetry. The horrendous event that occurred that day—the assault on the U.S. Capitol by an insurrectionary mob—terrified and saddened me. Like so many others, my faith in my fellow citizens was deeply damaged. How could we be so divided, how could our country have fallen into such mayhem? And how were we ever to come back from the abyss on which our nation teetered?

    Heart-broken and despondent, I returned to Lisa's manuscript and there, in the refuge of her words, I found solace and strength. *Truths and Consequences* tells the story of how the human spirit can be battered. Without artifice or piteous sentimentality, Lisa lays bare the facts of her life, the ordinary cruelty that lurks on an abandoned hillside, that resides behind "the [broken] screen door, the blue and white dishes." She spares her reader nothing, but rather demands that they, like her, serve as witness to the suffering caused by one individual to another. She requires us to stand in her place, recoil from the blows on her body, feel the rage that erupts, and know that it is completely justified.

But then—because, at essence, Lisa believes in the power inherent in all living things—she takes us through a journey of healing, which is defined, at its root, by the potency of love. We are communally healed as she receives the love offered by her "working man's hands", as she announces, "this love is thick." We are guests at the feast that she sits down to, and we are glad for her.

It would be a mistake, however, to think that this is a fairy tale ending, that the prince saves her from the ogre's clutches and they live happily ever after. Lisa is too wise for that; hers were lessons that can never be erased. In the final section of *Truths and Consequences*, Lisa continues to chart, as she must, her own story, her own path. Though now accompanied, she remains committed to her freedom, and still navigates her life according to her own inner compass. With grace and poise, using imagery and language that stuns and shines, Lisa documents her day-to-day understandings of a world where the consequences of a life can lead to a wealth of truths. And we, her readers—invited to walk beside her and bear witness with her—are gifted with "a clear view of the western sky". And it is good.

    H. Ní Aódagaín
        Murphy, Oregon
        January, 2021

I

Written Dissections

Biology

I knew she wouldn't approve
so I kept my work confidential—
nine lizards and one shrew,
gifts from the well-fed cat,
dissected, examined,
pinned on pads of corrugated cardboard,
organs and some bones labeled
with all the professional care
a 10-year-old could muster,
safely and neatly stowed
in the secret box in the back
corner of my dark closet.

My studies somehow had over-powered
the smell of mothballs,
the main odor of the house
in the shade of Sloan Mountain.
    "What were you thinking?"
my mother demanded
as she pulled one scientific model
after another, all ten of them,
out of the closet and into a garbage sack.
    "I was thinking I might learn something,"
I grumbled, which brought a swift rebuke:
    "Don't you get smart with me!" she snapped,
gagging a little from the stench
of decaying wildlife.

Over the years I have wondered
about the irony in her words,
about my sudden loss of interest
in biology, and my turn toward
cleaner endeavors and written dissections,
ideas about the natural world
but not the world itself.

Mrs. Ruby on playground duty in May

She saw me sitting alone
again, during recess, in the shade
of the library's eaves,
my back against the wall,
my nose in a book
again, and she approached
very gently, very earnestly
concerned for my well being.

She interrupted me in my silence,
her words yanking me from
the thunderous action of *The South Pacific*
(Book Five of the <u>High Seas Adventure Series</u>),
urging me to abandon ship to
   "join in with the other girls"
who were grouped around the swings
again, pretending to ignore the boys
on the monkey bars. Again.

   "No thanks," I said. "I just want to finish."
I tipped my open book in her direction,
and returned my nose to its normal place.

   "You know, boys don't like smart girls,
   girls smarter than them. You know that,
   don't you?"

Well, I was dumb-founded.

   "No, I didn't know that" —

Her teacherly face brightened,
sensing a break-through—

   "but that sure explains a lot," I said

thinking about the attention
the boys dumped on Tiffany and Deb
when they came over from the Special Ed Room
for PE and Art.

   "Explains a lot?" she squeezed out
of her receding face, unmasking
the look of one about to give up.
     "I don't like the dumb boys, Mrs. Ruby.
     I like books."

I could have thrown her a bone, I guess,
and I might have if she hadn't
huffed, turned, and marched away
in her low-heeled navy blue pumps.

Moon Mission

When Neil Armstrong walked on the moon,
I was eight and suddenly obsessed
with everything Apollo. Everything.
I pestered my family with questions
and annoyed them with the answers—
I read every bit of every news article
that came into the house. I clipped
charts and diagrams and moon maps
and taped them to my closet door.
I wrote a letter to Walter Cronkite,
the authority on the Apollo program,
asking about the astronauts' quarantine.
I received a nice reply from Mr. Cronkite
encouraging me to keep up with my studies
and referring me to NASA for an answer.
I wrote to NASA, too. They didn't write back.

Less than a year later, after Apollo 12
had made it to the Ocean of Storms
and back, my attention was laser-focused
on Apollo 13 and Fra Mauro.
Fra Mauro. I imagined a place
as beautiful as its name.
TV coverage of Apollo 13 was terrible.
I griped to my mom who logically noted
"people may have lost interest—
it's the third moon mission in nine months!"
People are stupid, I grumbled.

After the explosion,
coverage was everywhere.

Everywhere around the world,
people took note. No detail went unreported
as smart, creative scientists figured
how to remodel a spacecraft in space
and get the crew back to Earth alive.
This was huge, probably impossible.
Math was never more interesting.

After the peril was over, the lunar module
lifeboat bobbing in the Pacific,
the joy in the world was palpable;
pride in a hard job heroically done
spread like a welcome contagion.
I spent days saying "Fra Mauro"
just to hear it said. I spent years
feeling proud of my country
where education was valued, and
out-of-the-box thinking encouraged,
where a good idea could take off
like a rocket and change the world forever.

KBEX 9663—Do you copy?

Saturdays got a lot more interesting
in the early '70s,
when my dad took an interest in CB radios
and began setting up our family
home and auto emergency communication system.
He put a CB in every vehicle
and a base station in the kitchen.
Due to my older siblings' adept
evasive maneuvers, I was trained
to man the base station
and help Dad test the range
of every CB in our system.

Saturdays scattered throughout
my childhood took shape
around my father's excursions
that came to be known as "CB tests."
I loved them. I was useful.
Dad would head out in his truck
with a new radio to try out,
and every few miles, he'd call in:
    KBEX 9663 to base—do you copy?
    Base to Super Ten—copy, loud and clear.
He'd report his location
    Just crossed the Applegate Bridge
and his intended next stop
    Think I'll head up Shan Creek.
    Roger, Super Ten.
A few miles further on, he called again
    KBEX 9663 to base—how's the signal?
    Sounds good, Super Ten
and so it went.

Sometimes after dinner,
he'd get out the map
and we'd sit together at the table.
His thick finger traced the radio test route,
pointing out his call-in stops,
teaching me to read the topography,
showing me the draws and saddles
> *that let the signal through*
and the hidden valleys and canyon walls
> *that stopped it short.*

Dad bought a lot of radios in the '70s,
regularly upgrading the system
with new and better gear,
all needing to be tested.
> *Let's see what the range is on this one*
In 1974, he installed a 40-foot antenna
on the roof of our house.
and boosted the range on them all.
It was a real game-changer.

I've come to see that manning the base station
through my teenage years saved my life.
Even now, a recurring dream begins
with my dad's voice crackling through CB static:
> *Super Ten to Base—Do you copy?*
Then dream magic opens a map
and we sit together, tracing with our fingers
the routes I've been traveling since he passed
and dream magic comes through
the draws and saddles
to close the distance between us.

Be A Hero

Lie to her.
Tell her she can be
whoever and whatever
she wants to be.
Tell her she matters
as much as her brother,
as much as anyone,
that masculine nouns and pronouns
(all men are created equal)
are gender neutral.
Perpetuate that lie. Lie
about her individual power,
tell her she is in charge
of herself, her choices,
her body.
Tell her not the truth
about a culture
that presses her to view
her body
as her commodity.
Lie to give her
room to breathe,
time to imagine herself
as worthy before
she has to fade
to background noise.
Tell her all a human child
needs to hear and keep
your bitter truth to yourself.
She'll see soon enough.

Early Bloomers

The true beauty of the crocus
is its brevity (It's a hit-and-run)
and its early I-like-to-be-first arrival,
harbinger of the good days to come,
the riot of color yet to come,
pushing the season like the girls
of April breaking out their short-
shorts and tiny tops far too soon.
Winter makes them desperate,
the flowers, I mean, for light
and warmth
and life in full bloom.

II

Bearing Witness

Witness

Tell your story Tell it right
To no one at first
But the sparrows in the trees
And the river on its way

To no one at first
Yet there will come a better time
For the river on its way
Washes sorrow out to sea

So there will come a better time
To open yourself under a clearing sky
Send your sorrow out to sea
Heal yourself in plain sight

Open yourself under a bluer sky
With the sparrows in the trees
Heal yourself in plain sight
Tell your story   Tell it right

Carnival

Her knees have buckled under and she is sunk.
How is it that she is unnaturally and suddenly supine
On the sloping riverbank, thickly overgrown with a tangle
Of kinnikinnick and blackberry vine?
She feels the crush of his weight and the forced calm
Of his voice—shut up, shut up—
As he fumbles and tugs, gropes and pulls.
Her teeth scrape against his hard-pressing palm
And she can see his squint and grimace
In the little light oozing through the tree line,
Splashes of carnival red thrown down
From the Ferris Wheel and Tilt-a-Whirl.
The grunts from this finishing boy commingle
With squeals of delight from the near distance,
Drifting down. Down he pushes her cheek
Into the cool ground, lurches awkwardly to his feet,
Stumbles away into the Spring night and carnival light.

Note to My Rapist

Blue balls aching and not a clue.
You did what they said, what you heard.
Ronnie said, "They all say no
at first 'cause that's what they are told
is right but they all want it so
you have to fuck the bullshit
and jam it in there."

That's what you heard and
that's how it turned
and I never said a word.

Fourteen and still silly,
cracking myself up by inventing words
—Just learning how—
goofing around with friends. We said
boys like you were snarfs:
        Snarf [snarf] *n* **1**: one who sucks farts out of dead chickens;
        2: one who sniffs girls' bicycle seats (*syn*: QUARMA)

You were more snarfy than some
but you were not my enemy,
nor my friend,
just one of the boys from school.

He Lied

and spread it all over the school,
said she wanted it,
said she was all over him,
skanky and too fat
to really get it on.

She lied too, first at fourteen—
said she was fine,
said nothing's wrong
when in truth it was all wrong,
she was definitely not fine, yet
the longer she kept her mouth shut,
kept the truth penned up and quiet,
the more impossible it became to speak
at all. And so it went
for thirty years.

Why I Didn't Report

I didn't report
because my mother was angry with me for being late
because I didn't understand what had happened
because he was a popular boy at school
because I hurt in all my private spaces
because I didn't know who to tell or how to tell it

I didn't report
how I couldn't move out from under him
how my teeth scraped against his hard palm over my mouth
how the brush on the riverbank stabbed my summer skin
how the screams from the carnival carried through the treeline
how his heavy breath smelled of beer
how I cried without sound

I didn't report
because I was fourteen and traumatized
because I felt ashamed and diminished
because I felt safer when I kept silent
because the world carried on anyway
because the world carried on
because the world

Lost Things

I lost my virginity
too soon, too soon,
—unwillingly—
and the powers
I lost with it:
lost my confidence,
       and feeling safe in the world,
lost my sense of direction
       and purpose,
lost my way.
It's something
I would like to get back
— not the virginity —
but the innocence
that should have been
mine for longer than 14 years.
Lost at a time when
the world was changing
too fast, too fast becoming
more brutal,
threatening and hostile,
lost before I learned
about romance and kisses,
tender touch and gentle care.
       I've learned to survive
as a casualty of the patriarchy,
as damaged goods,
as someone less than whole,
as a snuffed out candle
       that never brightly shined,
as a hidden truth,
a walking lie,
a witness.

Draft Field Guide for American Girls

We won't lie to you, Girl.
We are here in tricky times,
Treading tricky ground.
Learn to read the lay of the land.
Learn to use a field guide.
Learn. Start by knowing that
There are many good men
And there are many other kinds.
Learn to distinguish sub-species.

Use caution around the loud ones.
Their self-serving noise will over-power
You first, then unwelcome intrusions will follow.
    You'll hear these men
    before you see them,
    smell them after they leave.

Don't trust too quickly the eloquent ones.
Their poetry seduces and softens their lies.
They will talk you out of your self.
    You'll feel these men
    before you touch them,
    carry them after they're gone.

Let the wanderers wander,
Let the needy ones need.
Your work is not their keep.

You must care for you and do
All you can to shield
Your true self and discerning eye
In a culture that would put you down.
Learn the tricks before you take the field.
Learn. Then stand your ground.

III

Lessons from the World of Men

A Tale from the End of Decency

I'm going to tell it,
spill it, turn it over,
split the belly,
open it up
and kill it.
Do an autopsy on it,
an autopsy of this tale.
I'm a coroner with a table.
I'm a chef with a clean knife,
blade sharpened to a fare-thee-well.

Fare thee well
and tell it. Tell it well,
ring the bell, let it wail
on its own breath,
self-generated wind
in billowing sails
and the rigging clanging 'gainst the mast,
and the ocean swelling 'neath the hull,
and the hull cracking,
split like a nutshell
spilling out its meat.

White sheet on a washed-up shore
a washed-out whore,
a beach and a bitch
and a shipwrecked poem
with a minus rhyme from another
time-warped wormhole
where stars can't shine,
light held captive as an audience
of polite women who will not

walk out on anyone
with the eyes to spot
one true thing
and the tongue to
tell it, spill it, turn it over,
kill it.

Back Word Scenes

The morning sun squints through
a break in the window blind.
Stale air rises in heavy breaths
from yesterday's mistake
still sleeping beside me.
The acrid taste of familiar regret,
and in the background, birdsong.

Low hanging drips of Spanish moss
conceal any clear way through
this tangled old backwater.
Guilt-laden clouds, like stones
bury the possibility of hope. Here
there is nothing worth saving.

The child binds us to one
another, as does your incessant presence.
Somewhere in the back of my mind
I remember loving you.

I can take in the whole meaning
and full impact of your backhanded
retort. Salty-sweet blood oozes
into my swollen mouth. It's a sermon
only you can deliver, my love.

I never dreamed you
might make me
wait, ease me down, settle me down.
It is good you have gone
where you cannot hear me
pleading: come back, come back,
on my sorry knees crying, come back.

Name It

The Dogon people have a word for it —
Nommo — the power of naming, the power of a word
like the creation myths of old;
once named, spoken, called into being
the Word becomes manifest,
the flesh and bones of the world take shape.

Name it with a single word
and in a single mention
assert a god's power and create
a singular reality in the mind.

    Say *Home* and you can see it
in your mind's eye and feel
its particular vibe. Inhale its breath,
familiar, melancholy and somehow
always wrapped in blue sky.

    Say *Desire* and now your blood wells up
pushing your heart into your throat.
Follow with *Loss* and you feel not so much
your heart in your throat, but more often
feel the empty space left behind
your sternum, vacant but never silent,
sounding the perpetual echo of what was
once named
Love.

Broken up

He meant to break her in two.
He breaks her, too. He is
breaking them in two.

What is broken?
The screen door,
the blue and white dishes,
belief in words,
the comfort of home.

She almost got used to it.
She got used.   It used to be
a rare occurrence of limited velocity
and fast-healing wounds.
She used what she had to clean up.

It used to be like this.

He cleaned her clock on Sundays.
Most often, she cleaned up after
with blue and white bar towels
and apologetic words.
He took after her now like clockwork,
like clock hands ticking off
the hours in the dark.

Dark nights conceal bluish wounds
and old scars that break open anew,
broken—healed—broken.
Broke.

Valentine to Myself

I wanted to say I love you
or say you are loved
even if you never have
felt it and even if the one
you thought you loved
said he loved you most,
loved you more
than the women you
have smelled on his shirt
and in his beard,
even if you thought
love was patient,
thought love was kind,
you never felt it
like that at all,
never felt it
strong and clear,
sharp as the sting of a backhand,
serious as a shove down the stairs,
so I wanted to say
you are loved
and I love you
but the lie wouldn't pass
over my swollen lip.

How to Poison Your Lover

Fuck him first.
Then whisper into the open
Capillaries of doubt
And the pulsing receptors of jealousy.
Ease into it. Get just a taste
And soon you'll be looking,
Really sniffing around for any trace
Of a weak spot. The way in
Is the way out. In no time
It's like tying off, like popping your last
Good vein, firing up a juiced load
Of accusation, bitter and snarling,
It burns and you can't resist
The way it courses through you.
Amped on anger, substantial as air,
Like scorched spun sugar dissolved
In a spoon and drawn through a pinhole.
It's a narrow escape indeed.
When it's too hot, turn up the heat.
When you've both had enough, go for more
Until you are hemorrhaging hate
From self-inflicted wounds too deep
For any loving to staunch.
Four or five words more to justify your running
And you are gone.
But fuck him first.

Survivor

So, what remains is just
this one
invisible wound.
Black goes blue.
The tender places
yellow, then unattended, fade.
Discolored pages in the story
I've been over
so many times
it no longer touches me.
The fear turns
to caution—slowly—
but it turns.
The fractured pieces
reassemble into something
stronger.
Echoes fall silent.
Even scars grow
eventually familiar enough
to become character.
Yes, the body recovers.
The body survives.

Lessons from the World of Men

1.
It is best to rise first and tidy
The tables and trailings from the night before,
Shoes to the closet,
Half-empty glasses to the sink.

2.
Keep your secrets in the dark,
Safe from probing tongues and bitter bites.
The need to know is a gluttonous maw,
A hunger best sated
With sweet and airy lies.

3.
Survival won't come easy
And it will never be enough,
But violent gusts that beat and blow
Are best settled with a fuck.

4.
Take care when you bury things:
Best to go deep if you want it
To stay gone.
Even the tightest tombs
May ooze malignant toxins
Into the cleanest rooms.

Fat Broad

She has been checked out for years
From her womanity, nearly divorced
From the body that betrayed her,
The body that made her vulnerable,
Made her victim.
Thick cloistered years spent
Swallowing fear until her head pounds,
Stuffing down the weight of gnawing pain,
Piling on armor in pasty layers
To encase not only her hurt but her heavy heart
In a corpulent cocoon.
Safe.
Separate.
Untouched.
(((invisible)))
The power of it astounds even her.

Still

It's a man's world, I know.
I feel it in the day-to-day trappings
of this American life, big things and small
like the discomfort in ill-fitting
breast-smashing seat belts,
in the dismissive condescension
of salesmen and preachers,
the discourteous speech patterns
of interrupting, winking windbags.
I feel it in the disservice
that comes with the default preference
for the penis in all matters
financial, governmental, and legal.

And yet I have never wanted
to be male--too much hanging
on every word, too many regrets
needing apology, too often worry
about when there will be retribution
and arsenic in the apple pie.

Violence Against Her

Why are the abusers always surprised
when the abused fight back?
The abused strike back
after years and centuries
of taking the hits, the body blows,
suffering mostly in silence
while under the surface
fuming,
blood boiling,
pressure building.

Really, it's the chronic abuse that fosters
a climate of cruelty
and backlash ever more brutal.

This is natural.

A battered wife reaches the point
when instead of using her hands
to shield herself, she uses her hands
to pick up a claw hammer
while he sleeps.

A suffering child grows
into a chef serving a cold dish
with a butcher's knife and a fist,
a superhero without a cape.

Beyond the tipping point of forbearance
the Living Earth strikes back,
rises up against her abusers,
with ferocious fires and smoke,
drowning and downing hurricanes,
blistering heat and drought,
invisible virus aloft and out of reach:

No hammer nor knife,
no superpower nor fist,
no surprise.
We cannot be surprised.

This is natural.

Waiting For the Light, I see my Ex

From the boxed-seat of my idling car
I watched him digging
in garbage piled on the ground
around the heaped-full dumpster.
I saw him pick out some
dark object and clean it
with his filthy t-shirt.
I could not see much more
from the distance of one left-turn lane.
I could see in his manner
as he held the artifact close for inspection
he had found something good.
Something like satisfaction, or perhaps,
victory straightened him to full height,
a tall point of reference, diminishing
for a block in my rear-view mirror.

Survival: A Field Guide

I might try living like the trees,
How they go on, layering the years,
Concealing the past.
Each season's accumulated woe
Is tucked under, barked over.

Survival is forgetting.

"Oh no," says the dendrochronologist.
"The rings are a record,
An unforgetting. The rings
Forbid forgetting. We see
Springs of great growth.
The meager years show, too,
But are dominated and encircled by the more vigorous ones.
It is fascinating to see the whole life,
Events recorded, history preserved."

An epic poem in wood.

But this is an unnatural view,
The living revealed by dying,
A life visible only in death.
On a standing tree, we see
Signs of age and character,
Scars like beauty marks, love knots,
Wounds, embellishments.
Here and there, the sap hardens.

Forgetting is merciful.
Forgetting is a holy word.

In the high branches, hear hope disintegrating,
Hear the sound of hearts breaking,
Of love failing.
What is the science of betrayal?

To be cut open, bisected,
With one's life laid out on exhibit,
A brazen display of history.
This open-book record-keeping obsession
With the facts kills.
One cannot live through such exposure.
Too much history is unbearable.
Forget about it.
Dress the wounds.
Layer upon layer.
Tuck under. Bark over.
Survive.

IV

Mother and Son

Thirty Years On

It was the only decision I could make,
the only path I could see
going in the right direction.
       And it wasn't really a choice
since choice suggests a viable alternative.
It was a decision to go on,
to move into an uncertain future,
and leave behind a miserable man
who had lost his way.
He took me with him for a stretch
and three times nearly ended me.
I was a naive coward and so I stayed
for nine intermittent years of
mindlessness,
homelessness,
fear and
self-loathing.

But when you came into existence
in my imagination and my womb—
an abstraction blossoming into a child,
a son growing inside me—
       I found my courage and knew:
We could not live in his misery.
We would not live.

Many counseled against single-parenting.
A few tried to shame me
       for being unmarried and pregnant.
Some suggested termination and waiting
       to start a family with a better man.

But I knew my family was already started.
      You were already here
in my world and loved.

It was the only decision I could rationally make,
and so I chose for both of us.

February 13, 1990

The night you were born
Ice-coated windows magnified
The sporadic snowfall
That materialized magically
Out of the black sky.
I remember the puffed squint
Of your new eyes meeting light
For the first time,
The tight bend
Of your untested legs
Shrinking away from spaciousness,
Your mottled skin glistening
With the dampness of newness.
And I remember
Drifting off to sleep
With your new breath
In my ear.

Existential Trinity

In the collision of intellect and emotion,
Divinity is born.
Feel the rise of life. Feel the sacred swell.
A boy begins as an idea,
A conception of some more golden tomorrow,
And Shine alone
Lights the way.

Strip away scarred skin;
Swirl and foam sullied flesh,
Back to the barren whiteness
Of the bones.
Flash white in the sun;
Wash slowly into fine
White sand
Brined at high tide.

To a seastack like a mussel cling:
Storms come and the wind
Carries salt.

For my fatherless son

Your mother loves you.
And the world is hard.
And you are mostly on your own,
Mostly lonely or alone.
It's a choice you make early on,
How you will bear
The circumstances of your birth,
How you will carry yourself and present
Your particular human flaws,
How you will hone and offer
Your particular human gifts.
It's a choice we all make
Not once but over and over
The mazey ways of our lifetimes,
Up to the circumstances of our deaths.
The world is hard.
And your mother loves you.

What a Woman Bears

She sets two places at the table—
Her own and one
For her only son—doubting
He will come home for dinner.
The absurdity of this hollow pretense
Compels her to repeat it.
Going through the motions of normalcy
Might shore up the façade of family
Long enough to become one again,
Long enough to save him.

And when he stumbles
Into the house, one more time
She looks past his heavy lids
To the eyes that first smiled at her
Eighteen years ago.
She hears under his incoherent words
Echoes of the boy she carried.
She is carrying him still.

How It Is

When I look at you, son, all grown up,
I see a history I do not want
to recall and cannot forget.
I wish I'd see loose July days
by the river, the heat of the canyon
competing with the heat of our bodies.
But I don't. I want to
feel the cool water,
not the back of his hand,
not a knife at my throat,
hear water moving, not scalding
words steeped in booze.

Looking at you, son, now a man before me,
what always strikes me
is some stale, bitter memory
of a kick down the stairs,
a shove to the wall—hand crushing my throat—
a mistake between my legs.

What mother says this to her son:
my history is the divide we never can cross.

None of this belongs to you—
except that face you bear:
your green eyes are the same
green eyes under the same
furred brow. You have
your father's face, colors, sounds, body.
The man you never met and always hate
stands here between us
battering our hearts, hardening
our hearts from his miserable grave.

Falling

When you go there,
My son, my one, my fragile open heart,
When you dive headlong
Into another bottle,
How deep are you down
When you can no longer see
A way out and you
Have an opening so narrow
You manage only
A peephole view through
A chink in the lonely mortar
Of this hand-wrought prison wall,
Letting shine only
A single beam of sunlight,
A peek of moonlight,
And how infrequently
A shooting star?

The world is aging around us
And beyond us.
Stars burn out and die
Leaving transient traces
Of light falling lucidly
Across a dark Western sky.

An Optimistic Mother

Optimism is believing you
Will fuck up again
But not quite as spectacularly
The next time or it might be
Thinking you will stop
Drinking to drunkenness
Before noon on most days

Optimism is continuing
To view this as temporary
As a phase, relentlessly
Looking forward to the day
When you've had a belly full
When you've had enough mornings
Too shaky to hold a glass
Of water before downing the first beer
Enough mornings retching emptiness
Enough morning mirrors reflecting
Black eyes, fat lips, bruises and
Contusions without histories
Enough mornings without memories
Of the night gone by

Optimism is believing you
Will get better
Tomorrow

For Nick, in your new home

Grow strong here.
Grow well.
Picture yourself near your big maple
under a buttermilk sky,
breathing in the familiar
scent of your newly planted
oregano and rosemary.
Listen to the song of the frogs.
Remember the silver light
that showed you the way here.
See the birds take flight
on strong, beautiful wings.
See them also come back
home each night to roost here.

Freedom

Freedom is the burden
that holds you down
or back—keeps you idle
with fear of failing

Sartre declared it:
We are not free
Not to be free

Freedom demands an action,
even if inaction

And not choosing is a choice.

We are not free
Not to be free.
Like it or not
You are free.
The most worrisome
burden of all

can't pack it away,
or stash in a box
on the dark closet shelf,
even though you are free
to put it there

can't deny it
like an uneven mole
or a nagging cough—

Because you are free
you are free

to fuck yourself up,
turn your life
inside out,

with every choice you make
or don't
with every decision you make
or hem and haw,

with every action and act,
every actor,

the fact is—
Freedom is a burden

V

Commiserate Hearts

Pity the Women

Pity the women who cannot resist
the men who rule and ruin their lives.
Stripped of their power, they ought to be pissed
but they're not. Dolled up as queens of their hives
they busy themselves with lies and false fronts;
packaged for cameras, their painted on smiles
cover the evil of their masters' foul stunts
no matter how cruel, no matter how vile.
Most of us hope that one or another
will somehow recall the taste of good will
and step up to help a sister or brother
but they don't. They go in for the kill.
    What makes a woman discard her own soul
    to service a man whose heart's a black hole?

Women's Work:
    (footwashers, cooks and incubators)

Religions are the enemy of the Good,
cultivating hate in the name of Love,
sowing fear of the unfamiliar Other
and intolerance for diverse Ideas,
codifying a tyrannical Patriarchy
meant to keep women Silent
and subservient, imposing Practices
of offensive dominion so Pervasive
they are accepted as Righteous
traditions to be joyously Passed
to our Daughters.

The Sacrifice of Hands

A well-lit display case in the downtown salon
Is full of right hands and wrists,
The acrylic nails painted in eye-popping colors
And sculpted to dysfunctional lengths,
Like garnished crabs in an interstellar fish market.
Some are striped, some squared-off pincers,
And all for sale! You too
Can have the two-inch box-tipped
Lime-green beauties. Go ahead. Splurge!
You deserve some extra sparkle.
You too can take your fully adorned
Crustacean-shaming claws
Into the world at large, and find yourself
Uneasy with keyboards, awkward with buttons.
Check your phone with dragonfly fingerlings!
Sport self-inflicted wiping wounds!
You too can be preciously polished
To prima donna perfection
And utterly disarming in your crippling beauty.
An incredible bargain at any price —
Hell, for something like that
You'd give your right hand.

Forest Crone

      It's been awhile since the children were here.
      Where have they gone? When might they come?
      The forest closes in with no company,
      no child to tend or care
      for. No one to cook
for. Years ago it was different.
Village women came by needing
forest respite from their labors at home.
Men came seeking comfort, for their wives
could not meet their needs.
And the children on some woodsy romp,
      but no more.
      It is a cold oven, most days.
      An empty table in a silent house.
Children bring their curious hearts
full of questions and joyful noise.
Women bring their commiserate hearts,
their pain wrapped in narrative.
Men bring their petrified hearts
and money to buy some softness.
      I have conjured what was needed. Yet
      misunderstood and fingered by tongue-waggers—
      witch, cannibal, lunatic, whore—
      my way is just to stay
      aloof under the roof of the trees
      in the quiet near dark water.
My door is open to all, but those who fear me
will likely stay in town. Those who know me
from the face in their mirror should come see.
Come out, come west, we'll sit together
and drink a distilled cup of truth.

Women in the Middle Ages

I remember the day my mother broke:
It is a Saturday in April 1974,
Laundry day, ordinary day.
The dining room table is covered
With the yellow fabric my sister chose
For her prom dress, pinned in tissue-thin
Pattern pieces arranged carefully to make
Frugal use of the over-priced material.

I don't remember what I said or did
Or asked or misunderstood so badly
On such an ordinary day
Or how I tripped over her
Stretched-to-the-limit, newly-menopausal nerves,
But she snapped, right there in the middle
Of Saturday chores, standing at the ironing board
Yelling, "That's it! I've had it!"

And I remember tears spilling and an outburst
Of the most bitter English crossed with
The most profane Greek I ever heard
Come from her mouth. And she is sobbing
(I can count on one hand the times
I saw my mother cry) And she is sinking
Into the nearest kitchen chair, still
Yelling, "Get out of here! Go outside! Get!"

I went on quiet feet, one eye over my shoulder.
I went not understanding, not knowing
For thirty years or more how hard,
How brutal the world is on women
Of a certain age, in the middle of it all,
How the burdens pile on, expectations wane,
And disillusionment cracks the will.

Old Testament: Book of Numbers

Last week, she remade math,
changing from base-ten to base-twelve
because decade and dozen both start with D
and even though nothing adds up right,
"It's always nice to have a couple extra,
isn't it?"

For two solid weeks last July,
she called her sister Fran twice a day,
mad as hell that she wouldn't pick up the phone.
"Isn't she ever at home?"
Fran died in 1999.

Misplaced zeroes in her check register
turned five grand into a half-million
and she insisted that either the bank
or the calculator was no good.
"Get me a new one," she said,
"with bigger buttons to handle
these bigger sums."

She took the battery out of her
left hearing aid because the TV was too loud
and put the little disc
in the Thursday box of her pill-minder.
On Friday, she felt "a little queasy"
and said "I can't hear a damn thing."

She keeps the microwave clock
10 minutes fast so it doesn't
overcook her broccoli.

Each new month brings new confusion:
the blank squares on the calendar
denote missing days. "Some scam,
no doubt, to cut social security."

Her days, missing and otherwise, roll
out and on in forgetful absurdity.
Nothing much happens. "Nothing
worth remembering."

A mention of "when
the kids were little"
takes her back in blue-sky clarity
to some sparkling yesterday in 1950.
Yet her children's children are
having children now, and she cannot
recall her own age.

Age assails and logic fails.
As logic fails, love prevails.

Terms of Endearment

Being an accident, as she called me,
Or at times, a mistake, I learned
Early on to earn affection
From my mother with clever language,
By polishing my words,
By using words too big for my mouth.
And I learned early on
Things get broken accidentally;
Mistakes are corrected or erased.
Yet if I had some merit,
Like some gift she might choose to keep,
If I could say the best words,
She might learn to love me.

When She Ended

In the cubicle behind the blue curtain
they asked me about her
mental acuity. *Lisa*, they said,
we need a starting point,
a point of reference, and began
prompting me with absurd questions:
Does she still read?
How about writing?
Does she cook her own meals?
Her life is in their hands
and they know nothing about her.
Yes, she reads every day, mostly
in English now but she has three other options.
Yes, she writes letters all the time, mostly
in Greek now but always in her small, beautiful script.
She cooks for herself and her neighbors
and what's left of her family.
She sews her own clothes, plants her own garden,
pays her own bills, keeps her own house.
She is strong, healthy, smart, talented.
She is on the gurney behind the blue curtain
unable to tell her own name.

To my mother in room R-11,
    Royal Gardens Nursing and Rehabilitation Center

Here I am again,
your youngest,
the one you didn't want,
the mistake you regretted, and delivered
with a mix of exhaustion and disgust;
another round of bottles and diapers,
and all that mess,
another mouth to feed,
body to bathe and clothe,
voice to tune out.
Five children? Really?
It's a grotesque absurdity.
I was chilled in your incubator
and you never warmed up.
See me here before you now,
still wanting
to be wanted,
yet settling
for your needy disdain.

October 4 in Room R-11

It's her 90th birthday,
Her first away from home,
Her last among the living.
As I do now every day,
I have come here straight
From work, bearing small offerings
Of comfort from home—
        lemon-scented hand lotion
        a piece of carrot cake
        two cards, mailed to me for her
        (one has a newsy letter from Electra!)
I hope they will please her.

Hi Mom. Happy birthday!
        What? Oh, it's you again

Her stroke-slurred words sound foreign.
The room phone rings and I help her
Pick up and hold the clunky handset

I hear my brother's voice—*Happy birthday, Mom!*
She lights up.
    Marc? Is that you?
Happy birthday!
        What? I'm here. I don't know where.
        What's-her-name is here again. That girl.
        I don't know—What's your name?
        I don't know
        I think she comes from the kitchen—
        Always with the food,
        Telling me to eat,

> *I don't know—*
> *Are you a cook? What's your name?*
> *Here, talk to Marc.*

She pushes the phone toward me.
I talk to my brother, tell him the latest.
> *She knew me yesterday,*
> *but not the day before.*
She's looking at me now,
A crooked smile of recognition
    or at least familiarity.
She asks me why I'm crying
    and calls me by name.

Pie

My mother started speaking to me again
on her 98th birthday. I was standing
at the kitchen sink, working the apples
like she did every Fall in my memory.

                Looks like you got a good yield
                off that little tree of yours
Yes, more than ever before
                Have you learned to
                make a decent pie, yet?
No, I quit trying
seven years ago
                Same time I quit trying?
Yes, I guess so.
                I kept going as long
                as I could stand.
Yes, I know
you were tired.
                I think we were all tired.
                I couldn't stand it anymore.
I understand.
                Dad came to get me.
                I looked up and there he was
                standing next to the bed
On your 68th anniversary.
                He never once forgot.
I won't ever forget.
                Oh, don't get all sappy on me.
                Get after those apples.
Ok, Mom, I'm trying.
                Try making a pie for Dad.
                He never met a pie he didn't like.

Gratitude in 2020

Think of the generations of women
who dwell inside you,
who make you
You.

Forget for now, for just one minute
the worry of the now,
the cancelled calendar now hanging
uselessly on the kitchen wall.

Forget all that
which is crippling you now
with fear, with uncertainty
and doubt about tomorrow.

Instead look back
to your mother,
your grandmothers
and their mothers before them.

Be grateful now to have
some of their skills,
some of their wisdom,
some of their strength.

Think of them
and remember:
You are the distillation
of their gifts.

Convocation: Women Grieve Together

A call comes
at an odd hour
from an unexpected caller
and you know before knowing
who? what? when? where?
and why, oh why?
something big has changed
someone dear needs help
and into this December
so full of ritual and rote tradition
we are called to our senses
to our conscious practices of love
we call forth our most tender stories
we tell them and call forth
the ghosts that lived them
filling an empty house
with the true ornaments of the time
our loved ones, our own
we call forth our ghosts
we tell our stories
and spend time again
in spirit with the love
that brought us here

Welcome to a New Daughter

You will speak your mother's tongue,
Learn her ways, live in her village.
We will feed you and teach you
All our mothers passed to us.

Learn our ways and honor the village
Here will always be your home
All our mothers showed us how
To be good keepers and speakers of love

Here you'll always have a home,
A final stop for every journey
A family of keepers and speakers of love
Makers of poems, singers of song

Come home at the end of your journey
We'll teach you, good daughter, feed you
Fierce poems and songs to be sung
You will speak your mothers' tongue

VI

The Sky is Sometimes Blue

Tempered Steel

He said she was beautiful
and she believed him,
just for the minute
she spent considering that
perhaps, underneath the accumulation
of years and scars,
under the façade of detachment
and practiced toughness,
below her cynical disbelief
in a potential for anything good,
beneath the weight of steeled nerves
hardened by an iron will to be
thought strong, independent,
even formidable,
there may be yet a remnant
of the girl she once was,
something lovely, still lovely
and alive.

Post-Meridian: January 17, 2012

We stand together
On the western edge of the continent,
Here to consider the first year
In the best half of my life,
Taking its measure by the foreseen
Treasure of our coming tomorrows.
In the mutual moments, we both know
This love is thick.
In water and light
The sky takes its sundown shape
In the colors of salmon flesh and fire,
Lit up like a mythic dragon's flight.
Beneath, on the rosy twilight ocean
A fishing boat, carrying mid-century rust,
Comes into harbor once again,
The steady chock-a-chock of the old engine
Mixing with the gulls
And the lullaby rocking of surf roar.
Evening unfolds before us.

Sestina: Leaving a Mark

We never know what kind of mark love leaves
Or how some scars become more tender in the light.
On the open prairie, how the sun comes down
In streaming bands to delineate and move
The long reaching arms of the sky,
To gather sheaves of timothy and rye grass.

Lying in your arms, in field grass,
Looking up through the silvered leaves
That splinter a flawlessly blue sky,
There is always an assurance of finding light,
In the turn of the Earth, the way you move,
How only your blue settles me down.

Your touch has the easy softness of down.
Your hair carries the air of cut grass.
To breathe you in is the surest move
To turn me. This time with you leaves
A lovely mark etched by the light
Coming out of your eyes, out of the sky.

Your hands could coax the blue out of the sky,
Roll it, knead it and lay it down,
Like a burden once heavy now light,
Like feet gone weary on stones finding grass.
Your tongue shaping my name leaves
Me restless and mute, needing only to move.

When the wind has a light hand, pooled water will move
In patchy ripples, like clouds in a buttermilk sky.
If time has a sound, it is the fluttering leaves
Of one true book, the pages thumbed gently down
To take in the fullness of Whitman's poems of grass:
"All swings around us—there is as much darkness as light."

What is hidden in the shadows is not unclouded by the light,
But nothing hides the sex in how you move,
Like wind engaging fields of ripened grass.
You smile for me and I recall the sky
Is sometimes blue. Love will not take us down,
But who knows about the mark it leaves?

With the blushing leaves, in the dropping light,
We will go down. We will so move.
But today, under this sky, only lay here in the grass.

One Chance More

You touch me and I learn
a new lesson:
a woman, broken and disfigured
may have one chance more
than her countless failures.

I feel the possibility
in the subtle warmth of your breath on my neck,
the ease of your callused hand under my breast,
the fit of our bodies
in wordless rhythm and rise.

Bring me to the truth of this
and I'll believe the taste of your skin,
the kindness in your eyes.

Logos
> *"The Word became flesh" (John 1:14)*

I want your mouth
To speak beauty into this ordinary time.
Say birdsong and I will hear
The trills of goldfinches chasing through green maples.
Call out the names of prairie grasses
And I will catch the wind sweetened
On new-mown hayfields in June.
Curl your tongue around summer sky
And I am wrapped in gold and light.
Say god and I feel my reason taken
In a rush down my spine,
Abducted by a particular pulsing need.
I want your mouth
To whisper primal secrets
Of fire-lit dances in the round
I want your mouth
To call my name.

I Do

I do
Hate this hounding.
You know the answer as well as
I do.
What free bird flies
Willingly into a cage?
Rather than archaic vows
Give me the poem that is your mouth.
Speak in depth with me
About nothing in particular
And everything that matters
In words that are your own.
If choice turns to commitment
Time becomes a trap.
I do
Want to taste the dreams that feed you
And crave to tell you
Wordlessly all I may become
In one luscious tangle
Of motion and hum.
Know the song that is you,
I want to, truly,
I do.

Map to You

This cartography is hard.
I have been working my way
Here for decades,
Charting my course
Through mostly hostile
Dark terrain.
I almost didn't make it,
Seeing your light
As I did
So late

Small Promises

The evening opens under the singing
Of frogs, awake now in the Spring-warmed ground.
Where the bees were—two weeks past—so earnestly
At work on a riot of blossoms—now small promises
Push off the last milky petals and shelter
In the minute brush line of spent stamens.
One perfect note comes out of the trees,
And like love spooned out in small measures,
Is plenty, is enough to hush the clamor
Of cold spites and bitter jealousies.
Even stubborn echoes fade to a stillness
So full I can hear new leaves unfolding,
And quiet my humming mind long enough
To conjure the velvet nap and yield
Of sun-filled pears on my tongue,
Evoke the memory and feel
Of your mouth knowing mine.

Sestina: For Tomorrow
>"Feathers fall around you.
>And show you the way to go."
>(Neil Young)

Have we come to the time when we no longer watch
Out for each other? Has our love gone to stone,
Hardened, seasoned, tolerating no further break?
Battered by betrayal carried on a crow's wing,
Swooping down in sudden flight from a high branch,
Leaving a trail as visible as conjured ghosts?

If we could release the history of our ghosts,
Learn some new ways to watch
Each other's backs, and find one sturdy branch,
Make small careful moves down this stone
Path, our love may once again take wing
And we, having bent, will not break.

Some pairs struggle and choose to take a break,
Thinking perhaps that time will ground their ghosts,
But at 10,000 feet, seven rows behind the wing,
The storm in the distance is only something to watch
While thinking of aging alone and words on a stone
And a black feather drifting from a branch.

Two crows caw, scolding us from the big branch
In the big maple that in big wind refuses to break.
Their dark eyes shine like polished stone,
Bright obsidian beads; they rekindle our ghosts,
Our accumulated loves who with you watch
As I find a feather, know its origin, know its wing.

You and I are of the same wing.
Our home perch is on one branch.
And in our days together we can watch
Our bond grow strong or see it break.
The air is heavy with the baggage and lies of ghosts,
The weight of the past, heavy like a stone.

If we turn our backs on loss, we turn the stone
To dust, the fine powder of a moth's wing,
A protecting coat, the prayer shawls of ghosts,
The wrap of bark enclosing every branch.
This storm, though rough, is not enough to break
Us if we take cover, hold tight, keep careful watch.

Let's release our ghosts, swing them from a high branch,
Let the Earth hold stone and the sky carry wing.
Let Love not break on our watch.

Parsing Love

Remember when Oprah made a mantra of it?
Love is a verb. Love is what you do.
Grammarians would concur but with a verbose quibble:
Love is primarily a noun, an abstract noun,
made manifest in the physical world by action,
the clear domain of verbs, transitive and
intransitive, passive and active.
      Irregular.
Those who would argue that
you cannot scribe it both ways
must not ponder love at all;
they lack subject-verb agreement.

You tell me every day that you love me,
and speaking the words is an action,
a verbal act of love.
You show me every day that you love me,
love verbified and enacted with every
- love note you leave for me to find
  on a napkin by our morning coffee;
- tender smile across the table
  for no diagrammable reason;
- transformed piece of salvaged lumber
  turned into a garden box;
- gentle embrace
  to settle down my panics;
- care-full drive
  to take me where I want to go;
- patient bearing
  of my silly, tortured lines.

Ode for My Working Man's Hands

Rough and gnarled,
tough with callus,
nicked and scarred,
discolored by bruise and time,
strong, rarely idle,
long, thick fingers curl
around an invisible wrench,
even while sleeping,
even when singing,
hard palm curves right
to cup my jawline,
love my face,
tender, steady,
my working man's hands,
rough and gnarled
and beautiful.

Going Nowhere, gladly

In another life, I might have
been the much-admired chef
in a well-lit Montreal patisserie
on Rue de Parcour where every little thing
is extraordinary and perfect as I
chat easily in fluent French
with a Greek accent. I could have

been the entertainment editor
for the L.A. Times, awash in comped
theater and concert tickets,
landing the most hard-to-get interviews
with artists whose work I love,
writing fresh, insightful essays
for my weekly (syndicated) column.

Of all the lives I may have lived
and all the places I might have gone,
I think this one is best:
this gentle, quiet life, this living—
this peaceful calming place, this farm—
this is where I belong, where I am whole,
how I must live, how I nourish my soul.
This life, this place on Earth, this is
everything and enough.

Sunday

A warm April morning
under a flawless blue sky
has the song sparrows singing
of nesting their young
between home deliveries
of moss and shed feathers,
in flight after flutter,
uplifted and prompted
by these lengthening days.

My morning unfolds gently
without a single anxious note.
There is time for birds today,
time for nests of gathered goods.
Today there is time for these wings.

Coming Back

I'll come back
As the capable wrench
In your familiar right hand,
As the neatly folded handkerchief
In your hip pocket,
Or the resonant tenor
In your hearty laugh.
I'll come back to be
Somewhere near you,
A part of you.
I'll come back
In all these ways I love
And you will hold me:
I'll be here, just under
Your buttoned shirt pocket
Where I have been sheltering
For years.

A Good Day

We go walking, and so often
You take my hand. It feels right.
The world settles down. No noise
Only birdsong and a breezy rustle
In newly unfurled cottonwood leaves.
With a startling rush, the neighbor's dog
Runs the feeding Canada Geese
In Tom's field, lifts the flock to flight
And I can hear the weight of reluctance
In the heavy beat of wings.
We watch together as the geese
Rise on impossible wings and clamoring air,
Sounding their grievance across the open prairie.
Your warm hand tightens slightly around mine
And having come to the end of our road,
My hand in yours, we amble home.

VII

Being

About Being Connected

Among many truths is one shared by all:
Beings physical and spiritual, temporal and spatial,
Connected in the common hum and
Drumming of life's pulsing thrum, we are
Energy, weaving webs and nets in strands of language.
Folding around us, it wraps us together
Gentling our fears with soft cradling words,
Holding us secure, a loom ordering threads of thought,
In language we find our common cloth.
Joule-endowed, our words convey our souls.
Kinetics keep our lives revolving, recombining
Like letters in our alphabet: individuals working jointly
Make meaning, carry ideas, weave stories,
Nurture our natural need to connect.
One score and six is all we have to
Perpetually rearrange, poetically remix.
Quicksilver-like, our language resists boundaries too
Rigid but blossoms in wide open fields
Sprinkled with yellow and pink shyness,
Tenuous and pale, like a mist about to lift,
Unveiling an understanding that transcends the words
Voicing our lives, urging us to be always
West of somewhere, at the edge, pulses racing.
Xenophanes of Colophon wrote it first: we are all one,
You, me, us, them, we, all
Zealously traveling on our spoken way.

Tap-Girl Saves the World

For a Superhero like me
the decision to act—to deploy my powers—
must not be taken lightly.
There is public safety to consider,
bystanders to consider, and of course,
the Earth-altering, course-correcting force
of my hard-soled golden tap shoes.
I might start to subdue the villain
first with a little soft-shoe shuffle,
just to let his guard down before
I let loose with a nerve-jangling
barrage of floor-cracking,
bone-splitting, ass-kicking stomps.
River dancers fall back, weeping.
Kung-fu fighters convert to peace-niks
singing Kumbaya and yielding to
the superior power of the Tap.
Watch your step.
Find your rhythm.
Dance the villain into joy.
Step down hard on the carved-in-stone
ideas of who is allowed
or not allowed to tap their own dynamo.
Dance is for everyone.
Dance is for everyone.
Dream of a world of dancers
empowered to dance their dance.

Identity Crisis

My identity has been stolen,
And while I know it's not a holy-shit,
Sky-is-falling crisis,
I just don't know how to feel about this.
I mean, Am I
Going to come across myself
At some unexpected time and place—
Not me but Faux Me—
And what if she is wearing those great shoes
I saw just yesterday at Macy's?
Those shoes absolutely screamed "Me!"
Those are my shoes,
And—good god—what if
My identity thief is a man—which of course would make
The shoe scenario less likely—unless, of course,
They're a cross-dressing Queen or something,
Which is not to say I have a problem
With Queens or cross-dressing—
My god, no—I think of my friend
Joseph (later Josephine) before the change
When we were just friends
With benefits, and I remember thinking
That sex with Joe was like making love
With a woman, except, of course,
For the cock, but Jesus, they knew the touch—
Which makes me wonder,
If my identity thief is a local,
Someone I might cross paths with,
And being willing, as I am,
If I end up screwing my thief,
Will it be like doing myself? Not
In a Love-for-One sort of way,

But a perfectly fitting doppelganger way,
And how weird would that be?
Practically incestual.
Certainly kinky.
Possibly criminal,
Like this identity theft shit.
I mean, Jesus Fucking Christ,
Is nothing sacred?

Not Forgotten

I have forgotten how to knit
    but I never forgot how to learn.
I have forgotten the route to Elk Lake
    but I never forgot the route home.
I never forgot how
    to make my saxophone growl
    or the hoot of a barn owl
    or a screech owl
    or a car screeching to a stop.
I have forgotten the color of your car
    but I will never forget
    how you drove it, racing us away
from the edge where we dared dangle
    and the tangled emotions
    that keep us moving today.

Out West

It was your silence that turned me
Out and away from the hollowness
Resounding through this empty place
We sometimes felt was home.
Along the beach road, walking away,
I know one bird on the wire
Is less alone than two
Perched yards apart.

A silent sea stack divides the Pacific
On the fulcrum of its presence,
Cuts a single swell into
Two urgent, shore-bound surges,
Movement rushed by solid stillness,
Water curved by rock,
Rock carved by moving water
Into the shapely hips of Earth's
Ripe daughter posing in the shallows alone.

I long for a pelagic life, unbound,
In the company of sooty terns
Alone to drown or rise
On some airborne mercy.

Scarred Heart:
    Reflections on a Good Rock Tilled up in the West Field

I think it must be
A Southwest road map:
Reticulating lines, straight to the edges
Of arroyos and blind mesas,
A petroglyphic record etched by
Flash-flooded, wash-out traumas,
Some deeper than others,
Some just traces worn in passing.
Here and there, the white
Slashes of some thing harder,
Torn open to the flesh of raw love.
I think it must be that
An entire chamber is gone,
Lopped-off lobe of heart,
A lacuna where trust was kept,
The ventricle of letting go
Enough to love.
I think it must be like that.

A Red Tide Blooms

I am Alice through the looking-glass
gathering my wits and weapons
to adapt to life under this
deranged and ruthless Red Queen.

I'll need more apples and berries,
more wine in my half-empty glass
to color the sunlight coming through it
into a ray of rosy hope.

I am Dorothy in Oz, trusting strangers,
searching for some answers or an exit,
safe passage back to Kansas
with a wish for home in stolen ruby shoes.

Amid ten-thousand fevered brows,
I'm angered. I'm endangered. I'm stumbling
through a field of poppies
succumbing like a child bride.

city

concrete, steel and glass canyons
full of people but little nature
manufactured light and processed air
sustain our basic function
but not our poetry.
   I am not made
to see stars only on the big screen
and smell florals only in macy's
   each day let me feel
cool earth under my feet
and hear birdsong come
out of old trees

Ode to the Internet in the Pandemic

Inanimate being, You mighty entity
where all life perpetually exists
as an accessible file, You are
a lifeline,
a choir of a billion voices,
an infinite web woven
of ones and naughts.
King-maker, Deal-breaker,
Prophet and Liar,
You connect me
to friends and other real people
I know and no longer see,
face to actual face.
You share thoughts of others
everywhere I go or think of going,
so I am always accompanied,
as much as I choose,
yet never more alone and lonely.
You perk me up
with tempting new recipes
and neat garden tricks,
breath-taking photos
and occasional laughs.
You keep me
informed and skeptical,
sometimes cynical,
wary and appalled
with the news of the world
beyond the farm,
my home,
my sheltering place on Earth
where I can unload the weight

of my worry for the World
Wide Web. I will
go check the garden,
tend to my flowers,
(take a picture or ten)
look for our hawks, and go
see what Jack is doing in his shop.

Carpe Diem: Friday, November 13

Superman's tattered cape is hung up in the scraggly
old cottonwood snag at the edge of our neighboring field,
and I think it must have been a wild black-eyed wind
to blow him and his cape out of the sky,
like the unhinged skull-knocker that blew in
this morning, scattering uncollected leaves
like airborne bones over field and forest.

And I think a day that started with a gun-shot crack
from a blown transformer in the dark morning hours
must be seized by the throat and ridden like a curve,
grasping without bias whatever miracle hand-hold you find.

I think sometimes mindlessness is
a necessity, a skill, a tool for survival
but it is not a matter
of choice, of silence, or even of will.
It takes more than will to still
this buzzing mind, so full
of shaggy, unconnected comprehensions,
of feathery vows and arrowhead promises.

I think I think too much, yet
there is some dignity in obedience
to my natural self, yielding to the hard-rock miner,
dirty and musky from time spent digging
for solid matter and pointed thoughts,
solid as stone cut from the quarry on Marble Mountain.

I think from there the fiercest loose-leaf winds
blow hardest down the North face and across
the open bottomland; time and death both
are quickened, faster than a speeding bullet.

211

This old house, now owned by strangers
stands remade, barely recognizable as the place
where I learned to read and write and reason,
learned to ride a bike, plant a seed, keep a secret.

The old house on the hilltop belongs now
by deed to a retired couple from California,
refugees, like so many, wanting
elbow room and a clean breath. Some irony

that among their first deeds as occupants
was the elimination of every tree
and source of oxygen around the house:
the Mother's Day tulip tree—
now RV parking;
the best-for-climbing flowering plum—
now a ground-level stump, a grave marker;
Fifty-year-old rhododendrons planted by family hands—
now an unobstructed view of the concrete foundation.
The old family room with its floor-to-ceiling
Dad-built bookcases is once again
a small two-car garage where, I think,
nobody goes to daydream.

This dear old house, keeper of my history
in the shadow of Sloan Mountain, has become
someone I used to know, unfamiliar now,
family ties twice removed,
artifacts dispersed in boxes.

Directions: How to Get to Where I Live Now

You must start on the high desert
and go west. Always go west,
toward the edge.

Leave the wide-open sky,
adjust to narrowed views,
cut short by mountains rising
so abruptly from the valley floor
they surely count as walls.

Get past the solitude of being
youngest in a big family
parented by too-busy people.

Go beyond the abuses
of teenaged self-medication
and self-loathing on the dead-
end Loop on the hilltop.

Turn left at the next corner—
the intersection of Faking It
and Making It, and step on it.

Keep going straight for a bit,
wrangle your way through nine years
of violence at home
and time without home.

When you reach the plateau,
fuel up. It's a long stretch
next, through the labored years

peopled with women and children
working alone and together
with mostly unspoken words.

When you have gone as far as that
road will take you, slow way down.
Come into the peace
of life on the farm now
with honeybees and honey,
and a clear view of the western sky.

Lightfall

Up early on this uncertain Sunday,
a dim pre-dawn half-light hangs
over the still sleeping pastures.
Then in the west, unexpected brightness
shines the crest of Page Mountain
out and beyond the nearest hills,
above a river of morning fog.
The beauty catches my breath.

A new day comes,
not all at once to all—
look up and out, look ahead and beyond
to the places touched by earliest light,
to where the light falls first.
Every day begins in darkness
that will not go on;
every darkness finally yields
to a breaking dawn.

Acknowledgements

Thanks to the editors of these publications where several of the poems in *Truths and Consequences* previously appeared.

Crosswinds Poetry Journal Volume III 2018 "Logos" (Crosswinds Poetry, 2018)
Encore Prize Poems 2020 "Draft Field Guide for the American Girl" (National Federation of State Poetry Societies, 2020)
From the Heart of the Applegate "Survival: A Field Guide" (Applegate Valley Community Newspaper, Inc., 2016)
Grants Pass Daily Courier "About Being Connected" (May 24, 2010)
Reading the River "Sestina: For Tomorrow" (Applegate Poets, 2018) previously titled "Sestina: In Flight"
Verseweavers, #15 "Sestina: Leaving a Mark" (Oregon Poetry Association, 2010)
Verseweavers, #19 "Out West" (Oregon Poetry Association, 2014)
WomanChrist, 30th Anniversary Edition "Welcome to a New Daughter" (Christin Lore Weber. CyberScribe Publications, 2018)

Gratitudes

With gratitude, thanks go out to all my friends and family who supported me over the years as I worked toward this moment—the publication of my first book of poetry and the launch of N8tive Run Press.

I extend special thanks to H. Ni Aodagain for her encouragement and her keen editing.

I also am grateful for the support I had from my wonderful Applegate Poets and from the good, old Pagan Warrior Poets.

Many thanks go, too, to Ryan Forsythe, of Left Fork Books, for his advice and guidance.

About the Poet

Lisa E Baldwin, a fifth-generation native Oregonian, has lived in the Lower Applegate community of Jerome Prairie since 1966. She is a writer, teacher and farmer who believes a good life is one steeped in poetry. Baldwin created and facilitated the 2018 *Poetry Alive!* workshops and *Something About Poetry 2019* and *2021* seminars for the Josephine Community Library, and is co-founder of the Poetry-in-the-Public-Square readings. She is past-president of the Oregon Poetry Association and a long-time chair of the statewide *Cascadia* Contest for Oregon's K-12 students, as well as an OPA liaison for the Oregon Poetry Collection housed in the Knight Library at the University of Oregon. Currently, as owner of N8tive Run Enterprises, she works as a poet and freelance writer, an editor and publisher, a teacher, literary consultant, and poetry evangelist. Baldwin is an active member of the Oregon poetry community. She also serves on the Board of Directors and the writing team for the Applegate Valley Community Newsmagazine. Her poetry has been published in the *Jefferson Journal, Crosswinds Poetry Journal, WomanChrist: 30th Anniversary Edition, The Applegater, Grants Pass Daily Courier,* several issues of *Verseweavers,* the *Encore Prize Poems 2020* and *2018,* and regional anthologies *From the Heart of the Applegate, Moments Before Midnight,* and *Reading the River.*

www.ingramcontent.com/pod-product-compliance
Lightning Source LLC
Chambersburg PA
CBHW021956290426
44108CB00012B/1087